Letts USE ICT YEAR 6

JILL JESSON

CONTENTS

Borders and backgrounds

Write Away!

Layout and style can be altered to suit the genre of the text

To see what the layout will look like before printing from **File** choose **Print preview**. Add a couple of returns if you need to space it out down the page. To make a card fold the printed paper to put the text and picture on the front.

Skills To Learn | Changing the layout to suit the text

Add a background.

1 Click `Format` .

2 Select `Document...` .

3 Select `Landscape` .

4 Click `OK` .

5 Click `File` .

6 Select `Borders and backgrounds...` .

7 Click `▼` to see the choices.

8 Select **present** and click `OK` .

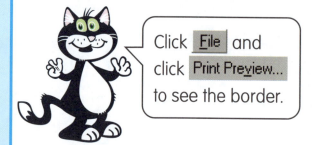

Click `File` and click `Print Preview...` to see the border.

Add some text.

1 In the font box `Arial` , click `▼` and choose a font you like.

2 Type Congratulations and tap `←Enter` eight times.

3 Type Max (or a name of your choice) and tap `←Enter` eight times.

4 Type with love from us all, and tap `←Enter` eight times.

5 Select all the text.

6 In the text size box `12 ▼`, click `▼` and select **24**.

7 Click `≡` to align text right.

8 Make the name size **48**.

Add a picture.

1 Click `Edit` and click `Insert` .

2 Select `Image...` .

3 Click `▼` and scroll down until you find a picture you like.

4 Click `OK` .

5 Select the picture.

6 Click `□` or `□` to enlarge or shrink the picture.

7 Add more pictures to the page.

8 Arrange them to fill up the spaces.

Click  to print your page out.

Lesson Link | English

Make a proverbs page.

1 Click Format . Select Document... .

2 Select Landscape .

3 Click OK .

4 Click Format , click Paper colour... and choose a paper colour.

5 Click OK .

6 Type some well-known sayings adding explanations about what they really mean.

7 Put them in blocks of text about half a page wide.

8 Click Edit and click Insert .

9 Select Image... and add clip art between the sayings. Use the align icons to set the text out in an interesting way.

10 Click ⬜ or ⬜ to make the pictures fit the space available.

Lesson Link | Technology

Fund raising poster design

1 Choose a suitable page layout, border and colour to suit the event.

2 Select a font which reflects the mood of the event.

3 Choose different sizes and fonts to fit each part of your message.

4 Use a border or add and resize art clips to make the poster attractive.

Off Screen

▶ Design a fund raising poster by hand and compare it with a computer designed one.

What are the advantages and disadvantages?

Special effects

PawPrints

Diagrams and text can be combined

Landscape layout is easy to use when making diagrams and flowcharts, since it matches the shape of most screens.

Skills To Learn | Developing presentation skills

Set page colour.

1 On a landscape page click ▶ and change the page colour.

2 Click ▢ , next to ◯ to choose a mix of colours.

3 Click ▶ next to Colour 1 .

4 Select a colour and click OK .

5 Do the same for a second colour.

6 Select a colour and click Top-Down or Left-Right to see the effect.

7 Click OK on your choice.

A water cycle poster

1 Use the line tools to make a circle of arrows.

2 Type The Water Cycle in a font which makes it stand out.

3 Use a small, plain font to explain each part of the water cycle.

4 Put each stage in a separate text box and moveto fit the space.

5 Select the list and click t .

6 Click 😐 to add bullets to the list.

7 Click 📷 , click Geography and add pictures to the poster.

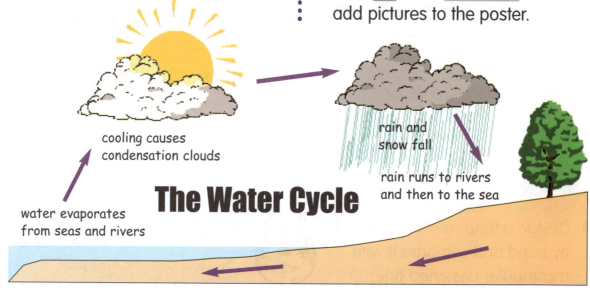

cooling causes condensation clouds

rain and snow fall

rain runs to rivers and then to the sea

water evaporates from seas and rivers

The Water Cycle

Lesson Link Science

A life cycle diagram

1 Use textboxes and arrows to show the stages in the life cycle of a butterfly.

2 Click to see the picture gallery.

3 Click `Science`, select `Animals` and add pictures to the diagram.

4 Click to print your diagram.

5 Muddle up the parts.

6 Click `File` and click `Save as` and save it as a template for someone else to re-order.

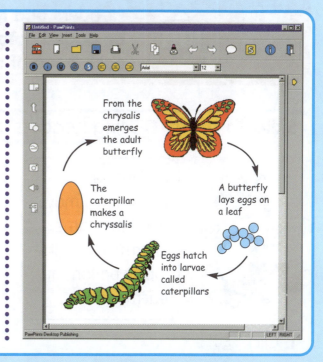

From the chrysalis emerges the adult butterfly

The caterpillar makes a chryssalis

A butterfly lays eggs on a leaf

Eggs hatch into larvae called caterpillars

Lesson Link History

Design a concept map.

1 Use arrows to link ideas in text boxes.

You use concept maps to show what you have learned.

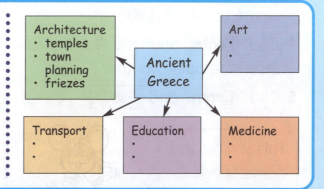

Architecture
• temples
• town planning
• friezes

Art
•
•

Ancient Greece

Transport
•
•

Education
•
•

Medicine
•
•

Off Screen

▶ Make concept maps by drawing your boxes on coloured paper.

▶ Add arrows and pictures to make the points memorable.

Use collage to make a life cycle and a water cycle chart.

Making templates

Write Away!

Headers and footers can be added automatically to each page of a document

Pupils may need reminding to use the spell check facility at this stage. Write Away does not allow the saving of a template in the way that PawPrints does. To get round this save a copy of the page you want for a template and then **Save As** each altered copy of it with a new file name.

Skills To Learn | Using headers and footers

Multipage documents may need the same information at the top or bottom of each page.

1 Click Edit .

2 Select Headers and Footers .

3 In the Header box type your name and click Left .

4 Click Footer and type #p to insert the page number.

5 Click Centre and OK .

This will put the correct page number on every page.

Click File and click Print Preview... to check what is in the header and footer.

6 At the top of the page type Title in a font you like and select it.

7 In the text size box 12 ▾, click ▾ and select **24**.

8 Click ≣ to centre it.

9 Tap ⏎Enter . Type Start here.

10 Click ≣ and then choose a smaller font.

11 Click 💾 and name your file Name+page.

Each time you want a named and numbered document open this one.

Alter the title. Delete Start here and start writing.

Add a frame to your text. Once you have finished click File , select Save As... and give it a new file name.

Lesson Link English

Make a letter template.

1 Click [new document icon] to start a new document.

2 Click Edit.

3 Select Headers and Footers.

4 In the **Header** box type #d to insert the date and click **Left**.

5 Click OK.

6 On the main page type the address at the top.

7 Select the address and click [align right icon].

8 Tap ↵Enter and type Dear.

9 Click [align left icon].

10 Click [save icon] and name your file Letter.

11 Save each completed letter with a new file name.

Use your letter template to write a letter to a friend or relative.

Lesson Link Technology

Start a recipe collection.

1 Click [new document icon] to start a new document.

2 Click Edit.

3 Select Headers and Footers.

4 In the **Header** box type the name of the collection, e.g. Delicious Dishes from Class Six.

5 Click **Footer** and type #p to insert the page number.

6 Click **Centre** and OK.

7 Type the recipes in the main page section.

8 Click [spell check icon] to check your spelling.

Off Screen

- Design your own headed notepaper with your own logo.
- Add your address in a fancy font.
- Add a decorative border.

Photocopy it and then complete each letter by hand.

Columns and links

PawPrints

Page layouts can include columns and linked pages

When making a document with a complex layout, it can be useful to add a grid of guide lines to a blank page to help line objects up in relation to each other. These guides are not fixed columns and text can be typed over them.

Skills To Learn | Using column guides for a planning sheet

Divide the page into columns.

1 Click `View` and click `Column guides`.

2 Use the arrows 🔼🔽 to set the number of `Rows` and `Columns`.

3 Select **3** in the `Columns` box.

4 Click `View column guides` to see the guides.

5 Click `X` to close the window.

To clear the layout guides, repeat the process, setting the values for rows and columns to **0**.

Add text to the columns.

1 Click in column 1 and type Introduction.

2 Click in column 2 and type some facts about wearing school uniform.

3 Double click to see the text box and drag it to fit column 2.

4 Click in column 3 and type some general phrases such as There is much controversy, or Many people think. Drag it to fit column 3.

5 In column 1 type Points for:-

6 In column 2 add notes about the reasons for wearing uniform.

7 Double click to see the text box and drag to fit column 2.

8 Click in column 3 and type useful sentence starts, e.g. Firstly, Secondly, Some children feel, Many parents believe, Another point, One advantage is… Drag it to fit column 3.

9 Plan the next section as Points against uniform and type some connectives you may need in the third column, e.g. which means, on the other hand, however, in order to…

Lesson Link   English

Write a strip cartoon story.

1 Click and select `Landscape`.

2 Click `Add a Page` to add two or three pages.

3 Click `View` and click `Column guides`.

4 Select **2** in the `Rows` box.

5 Select **3** in the `Columns` box.

6 Click `View column guides` and click `X` to close the window.

7 Tap `Ctrl` and **–** until you can see the whole page layout.

8 Add text and pictures to each section to tell a story.

Add page links to the story.

1 At the end of page 1 type Click here to read on.

2 Select Click here to read on.

3 Click `🗗` and select `🔗`.

4 Click `Go to a different page of this document`.

5 Click `OK`.

6 Type **2** in the `go to page number` box.

7 Click `OK`.

Now add links to all the pages to make a digital book.

Lesson Link   RE   F

Religion in the news

1 Use a three column guide to design a newspaper article on an important religious figure or event.

2 Write it as if you were there.

3 Use current newspapers for ideas.

4 Add pictures created in Fresco to add interest, or clip art from another source.

Think of a relevant name for your newspaper.

Off Screen

▶ Rule your own column guides to write brochures for health education leaflets.

▶ Draw a 2 x 4 grid on A3 paper and use this to write a storyboard or cartoon for a younger child.

Plan a slideshow

SlideShow

Learn to design multimedia pages

Pupils should be familiar with a range of multimedia programs so they can talk about the way buttons and icons are arranged consistently, how text size is used to indicate relative importance and how colours, text and graphics complement each other.

Skills To Learn | Making a slideshow with titles and graphics

1 Plan a slideshow about holidays.

Use the PawPrints holiday pictures for ideas.

2 Click **+** .

3 Click Text .

4 Click Enter a title... .

5 Click Font to choose the formatting options.

6 Click the Title . Type *Going on Holiday*.

7 Click OK .

8 Click **+** .

9 Click Picture .

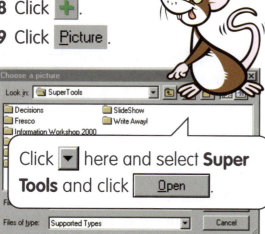

Click ▼ here and select **Super Tools** and click Open .

10 Select **PawPrints**.

11 Click OK .

12 Select **Pictures**.

13 Click OK .

14 Select **Holidays**.

15 Click OK .

16 Select the picture you want to add to your slideshow and click OK .

17 Add titles and pictures alternately to complete a slideshow about holidays.

18 Click View and select Display .

19 Click All Slides to see your slideshow.

20 Click the mouse to move between slides.

Press Escape to quit.

21 Click 💾 and name your file *Holiday*.

Lesson Link Science

Plan a slideshow to explain how plants reproduce.

1 Look at the pictures available in PawPrints and decide which you will need.

Click , click Science , and select Trees and flowers .

2 Open Slideshow and add text and pictures alternately to make a presentation on plant reproduction.

You can change the order of the slides.

3 Click View and select List .

4 Click on the slide you want to move and drag it to a new position in the list.

Or click View and select Storyboard and drag the slides into the preferred order.

Lesson Link Geography

Mountains presentation

1 Open PawPrints and click .

2 Click Geography and select Mountains .

3 Decide which pictures you want to use to make a presentation on mountains.

4 Make your slideshow.

5 Click Options .

6 Select Loop Slideshow .

7 Click View and select Display .

8 Click All Slides to see your slideshow.

Off Screen

▶ Plan a slideshow of work your class has done using Fresco.

▶ Write a caption for each piece of work explaining the ideas behind its creation.

Improve a slideshow

SlideShow

Slideshow sounds, graphics and text files can be added to a slideshow

Try these effects on the holiday slideshow already created. All text files to be imported into Slideshow must be saved as **RTF files**. Pupils should choose this option from the **save** menu when saving their work.

Skills To Learn   Adding special effects

1 Click File and select Open... .

2 Select **Holiday** and click Open .

3 Click View and select Storyboard .

4 Click the slide you want to modify and click ⭐ .

You can alter the colour and font of this text.

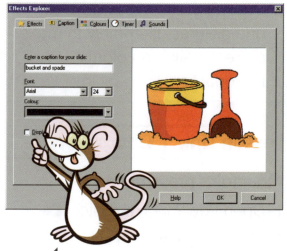

Click here to see the text on the slideshow.

Experiment with the effects available until you see the one you want. Then click OK .

5 Click Caption to add some text to a picture slide.

6 Choose Colours to alter the background colour of a slide.

7 Choose Timer to alter the time between slides.

8 Click Sounds and open a sound file to add one to a slide.

Lesson Link   Geography

Weather presentation

1 Use weather clips from PawPrints to make a weather slideshow.

2 Add sound effects such as wind, explode and dripping tap.

3 Record your own sound effects in PawPrints and add to the slideshow.

4 Add photos of weather conditions using a digital camera.

5 Add text about weather from Write Away and PawPrints files.

6 Click ➕ and select **T̲ext**.

7 Click ▾ and select **Super Tools**.

8 Click **O̲pen**.

9 Select **Write Away**.

10 Select the text file you want to add to your slideshow.

11 Click **OK**.

Lesson Link   Art

1 Click ➕ and select **P̲icture**.

2 Click ▾ and select **Super Tools**.

3 Click **O̲pen**.

4 Select **Fresco**.

5 Select the picture you want to add to your slideshow.

6 Click **OK**.

7 Click ➕ and select **T̲ext**.

8 Click **E̲nter a title...**.

9 Add title slides between each picture explaining the ideas behind it.

10 Click ⭐, select **Caption**, and add captions to each picture with its title and the name of the artist.

Off Screen

▶ Plan an art presentation using a flip chart, art pictures and models you have made.

▶ Write the text on the flip chart.

▶ Decide in which order the pictures and models will be shown and who will hold them.

▶ Make your presentation to another class.

Multimedia presentation

PawPrints

Diagrams can show the links between pages Buttons can link pages

Buttons to go to the next page should always go on the right of a screen. Buttons to go back should go on the left of the screen.

Skills To Learn | Planning linked pages

1 Click ▢▣.

2 Click `Add a Page` to add four pages.

3 Click on each page and type the titles, Start, 2D shapes, 3D shapes and Quiz.

4 On the top of the Start page type, To find out about 2D shapes, right click here.

5 Select the text.

6 Click ▣ and select ◉.

7 Click `Go to a different page of this document`.

8 Click `OK`.

9 Type 2 in the `go to page number` box.

10 Click `OK`.

When you RIGHT click the mouse on this text you will jump to the next page.

11 Use the diagram to help you link the rest of the pages.

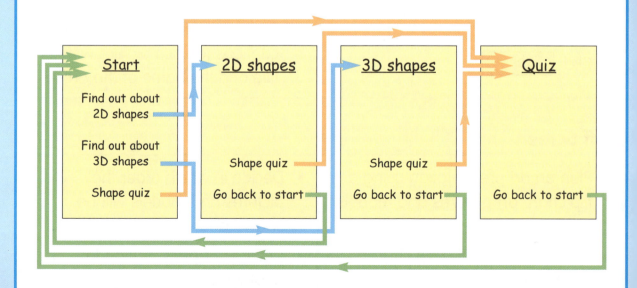

Lesson Link Maths

Add text and shapes to your maths presentation.

1 On the Start page add text explaining the difference between 2D and 3D shapes.

2 Click 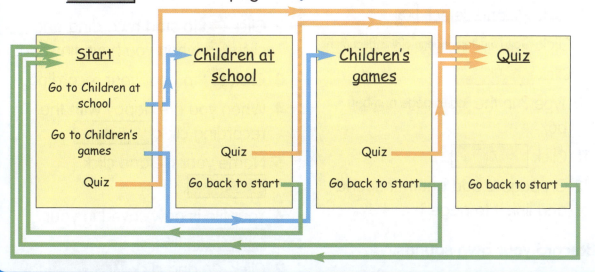 and add shapes to the Start page.

3 On the next two pages add text about the properties of 2D and 3D shapes.

4 Draw shapes and diagrams to illustrate each page.

5 On the last page write a quiz about shapes.

Lesson Link History

Children from history

1 Click .

2 Click Add a Page to add four pages.

3 Create a presentation on children in the past, e.g. Ancient Greece or Victorian times. It could look like this.

Start	Children at school	Children's games	Quiz
Go to Children at school			
Go to Children's games			
Quiz	Quiz	Quiz	
	Go back to start	Go back to start	Go back to start

Off Screen

‣ Draw a diagram to show how other pages could be linked to your history presentation.

‣ You could add a page on children's clothes, a 'Did you know?' page and a quiz page.

Adding sounds

PawPrints

A multimedia program can present information for a specific audience

Sound links are activated with a left click on the mouse.

Skills To Learn | Adding sounds

1 Click 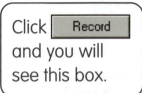.

2 Click Add a Page to add two pages.

3 Label them page 1 and page 2.

4 Click on page 1 and click 🔊.

5 Choose a sound and click OK.

6 Select the sound icon.

7 Click 🔧 and select 🔗.

8 Click Go to a different page of this document.

9 Click OK.

10 Type 2 in the go to page number box.

11 Click OK.

12 On page 2 add another sound and link it to page 1.

Record your own sounds.

You could record yourself reading the text on a page.

1 Click 🔊.

Click Record and you will see this box.

Record a sound ✕

Save

Cancel

2 Click ⦿ to start recording and click ✕ when you have finished.

3 Click ▷ to hear your recording.

4 When you are happy with the recording click Save.

5 Name your file and click Save.

6 Your file is now saved in your My Sounds file.

7 Click 🔊 and click My Sounds to browse your sounds.

Now you can add this sound to your work.

Lesson Link   English

Write a noisy story.

1 Click and add sounds to each page of your text.

2 Beside each sound icon add an instruction, e.g. Click to hear the car start.

> You could write Click here to see the next page.

3 Click , and add graphics from the clip art or from pictures you have drawn in Fresco.

Click here to hear the ambulance.

... Beth had a very important job. She was an ambulance driver. In fact she was the best ambulance driver ever.

4 You could add a sound recording of yourself reading the text on each page.

Lesson Link   Music

Compose percussion music.

1 Click ▢.

2 Click Add a Page and add five pages.

3 Click on page 1 and click ◁)).

4 Click Record.

5 Click ⦿ and play your music.

6 Click ✖ when you have finished.

7 Click ▷ to hear your recording.

8 Record each stage of the composition on a different page.

Add text and graphics.

1 Add text to say how you built up the music.

2 Explain what changes you made and why you made them.

3 Click ▢ and click General.

4 Click Instruments and add graphics of instruments and use them to link the pages.

5 Record the final composition on the last page of your document.

Off Screen

▸ Create a musical presentation about the different moods of the sea.

▸ You could include pictures, a poem and percussion.

Multimedia magazines

PawPrints

A multimedia program can present information for a specific audience

Ask the pupils to decide for whom they will make a presentation. They should consider the reading age and interests of their audience and plan a balance of text and pictures.

Skills To Learn — Planning a multimedia magazine

1 Plan off screen how the pages will be linked.

Try using sheets of paper for each screen page and pieces of wool to show the links.

Age – 8 year olds

Text – keep it simple

Ideas – like sport, making things, stories and poems.

Make notes about how you want the magazine to look, what age range it's for, and ideas to go in it.

2 Design each page on screen using PawPrints.

3 Paste graphs, pictures, photos and maps from other Black Cat programs or the internet.

4 Link the pages with sound clips.

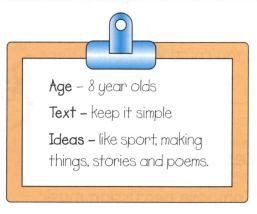

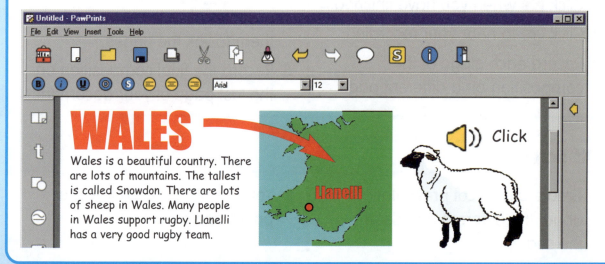

WALES

Wales is a beautiful country. There are lots of mountains. The tallest is called Snowdon. There are lots of sheep in Wales. Many people in Wales support rugby. Llanelli has a very good rugby team.

Llanelli

Click

Lesson Link | Science

Healthy living presentation

1 Include healthy diets, keeping fit, legal drugs and illegal drugs.

2 You could link like this:

3 Ask your parents for ideas to improve the presentation.

4 Make the changes if necessary.

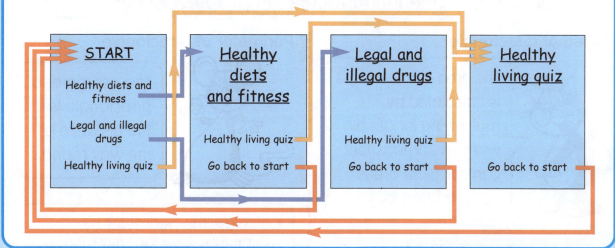

Lesson Link | Technology

Multimedia Make and Do magazine

1 Use ideas from the technology lessons you have had over the last four/six years.

2 Link the pages so that each one is linked to the Start page as well as to one or two other pages.

3 Add sounds, and pictures you have taken or scanned in.

Try to make it simple, but interesting enough to appeal to all age groups in your school.

Off Screen

▶ Draw diagrams to show how the pages of each presentation are linked.

▶ Use these diagrams to improve the links, and to help you link in new pages.

Using formulae

 NumberBox 2

Formulae can do calculations automatically

The spreadsheets should be discussed, copied and completed by the pupils. The modelling involves altering the numbers to see the effect.

Skills To Learn | Entering formulae into a spreadsheet

Area of a rectangle

The area of a rectangle is calculated by multiplying length by width. A spreadsheet can calculate areas using a formula.

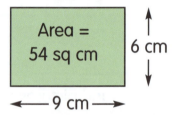

Area = 54 sq cm

6 cm

← 9 cm →

1 Click Start a new blank spreadsheet .

2 Click OK .

3 Type the length in A2.

4 Type the width in B2.

5 Type = in C2.

6 Click in A2 and click ✕ .

7 Click in B2 and click ✓ .

8 Change the length and width and see the result in each of the formula cells.

Perimeter of a rectangle

The perimeter of a rectangle is the distance all the way round.

Calculate the perimeter by doubling the length, doubling the width and adding the result.

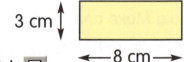

3 cm

← 8 cm →

1 Click ☐ .

2 Type the length in A2.

3 Type the width in B2.

4 Type = in C2.

5 Click in A2 and click ✕ 2 .

6 Click + and click in B2.

7 Click ✕ 2 and click ✓ .

8 Change the length and width and see the result in each of the formula cells.

Lesson Link Maths

Area of a triangle

The area of a triangle is calculated by multiplying the height by the base and dividing the result by two.

1 Click 🔲.

2 Type the height in A2.

3 Type the base in B2.

4 Type = in C2.

5 Click in A2 and click ✕.

6 Click in B2 and click ✓.

7 Type = in D2.

8 Click in C2 and click / 2 ✓.

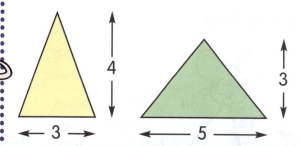

Lesson Link Science

Are shoe size and height connected?

1 Measure the height of ten friends.

2 Ask their shoe size.

3 Divide height by shoe size in a spreadsheet.

If there is a connection, the answer will be nearly the same each time.

4 Are there any two body measurements which you think will be connected?

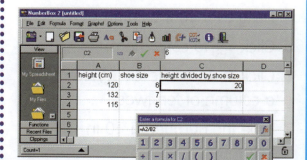

Off Screen

▶ Measure the perimeters of circles using a piece of string.

▶ Measure the radius of each.

▶ Use a calculator to check if there is a connection between the two measurements.

Tables

NumberBox 2

Formulae can be copied from one cell to another

Explain to the pupils that when they cut a section of text it stays in the computer's memory until another item is copied. This does not happen when they use the delete key.

Skills To Learn | Copy formulae from one cell to another

Times table

You can design a spreadsheet which knows all the answers to your times tables.

1 Click Start a new blank spreadsheet .

2 Click OK .

3 Type 2 five times in column A.

4 Drag over your column of twos.

5 Click to copy them.

6 Click in A6 and click to make a column of ten twos.

7 Type the numbers 1–10 in column B.

8 Click in C1 and type =.

9 Click in A1 and click ×.

10 Click in B1 and click ✓.

11 Click in cell C1 and click .

12 Click in C2 and click .

---

13 Click in each cell in column C.

The program knows to change the formula to match the row it is in.

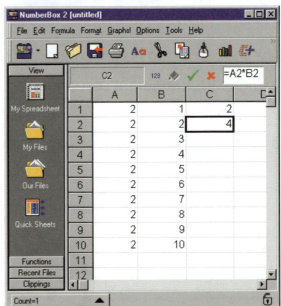

Change all the numbers in column A to 5, to see the five times table.

22

Lesson Link | Maths

Foreign exchange

Here is a holiday money converter.

	A	B	C	D
1	Currency you want to use	Number of pounds	Rate of exchange	Amount of foreign currency
2	Euro		1.55	
3	BAht		62	
4	Dollars (US)		1.43	
5	Turkey		1900000	
6	Mexico		13	
7	Indonesia		14500	
8	Singapore		26	
9				

1 Click in D2 and type **=**.

2 Click in B2 and click ✖.

3 Click in C2 and click ✔.

4 Paste the formula from D2 into the rest of column D.

5 Design a spreadsheet to do this for different amounts.

Type in the number of pounds you want to change and the spreadsheet will do the rest. Use a decimal point to type in pence.

Design a formula to paste into column E that knocks off 3% in commission!

Lesson Link | Geography

Convert feet into metres.

1 Copy this spreadsheet.

	A	B	C
1	Name of feature	Height in feet	Height in metres
2	Everest	29028	
3	Ben Nevis	4408	
4	Angel Falls	3212	
5	Deepest ocean trench	35797	
6			

Divide the number of feet by 3.28 to convert to metres.

2 Click in C2 and type **=**.

3 Click in B2 and click ╱.

4 Type **3.28** and click ✔.

5 Design a spreadsheet to convert kilometres to miles.

Off Screen

▶ Use a calculator to convert Celsius to Fahrenheit.

Leagues

NumberBox 2

Spreadsheet calculations can use brackets

Where two teams have the same number of points goal difference is used. Goal difference takes goals against away from goals scored.

Skills To Learn Using formulae in spreadsheet calculations

Goal difference

1 Use a spreadsheet like this to work out goal differences for teams you support.

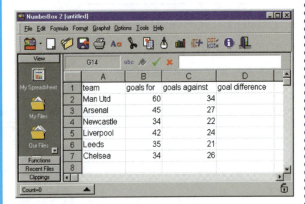

2 Click in D2 and type **=**.

3 Click in B2 and click ⊟.

4 Click in C2 and click ✓.

5 Paste the formula from D2 into the rest of column D.

If you enjoy watching goals which team should you follow? Add a formula and paste it into column E to find out.

Premiership points

Teams get 3 points for a win and 1 point for a draw.

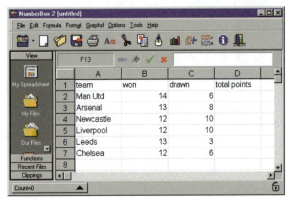

1 Copy this spreadsheet showing wins and draws for each top team.

2 Click in C2 and type **=**.

3 Type **(C2*3)+D2** and click ✓.

4 Copy the formula for working out the points total for each team.

For your favourite teams

1 Make a spreadsheet with the records of your favourite teams in cricket, netball or hockey.

Lesson Link   Maths

Percentages

1 A percentage is worked out in two steps,
- divide the number by 100
- multiply by the percentage.

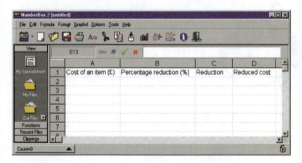

> Copy this table and use it to work out how much an item costs after it has been reduced in the sales.

Calculate £3.50 reduced by 10%.

1 Type **3.50** in cell A2.

2 Type **10** in cell B2.

3 Type **=** in cell C2.

4 Type **(A2/100)*B2** and click .

5 Click in D2 and type **=**.

6 Type **A2-C2** and click ✔.

> You need the brackets so the computer will work out what one percent is first.

7 Work out the new cost of:
- £2.20 reduced by 5%
- £7.20 reduced by 12%.

Lesson Link   PE

Team records

1 Make a league table showing the position of each rounders team.

2 There are 4 points for a win and 1 point for a draw.

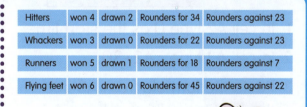

Hitters	won 4	drawn 2	Rounders for 34	Rounders against 23
Whackers	won 3	drawn 0	Rounders for 22	Rounders against 23
Runners	won 5	drawn 1	Rounders for 18	Rounders against 7
Flying feet	won 6	drawn 0	Rounders for 45	Rounders against 22

Off Screen

▶ Do more calculations which need brackets.

▶ Work out sale reductions in your head starting with 10% reductions.

Graphing

NumberBox 2

Spreadsheets can be used to produce graphs

These activities model biological growth, population growth and the pattern produced by square numbers.

Skills To Learn | Use a spreadsheet to produce a line graph

Micro-organisms

In perfect conditions the numbers of some bacteria can double every 30 minutes.

This formula shows that each generation of bacteria doubles.

7 Select all the numbers in the chart.

8 Click 📊 and 📈 to see a line graph.

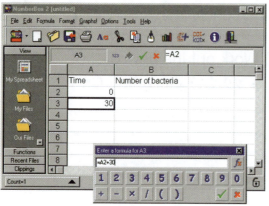

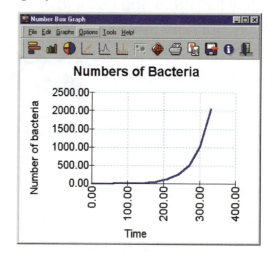

1 In cell A2 type **0** as the start time.

2 In cell A3 type **=A2+30**.

3 Paste the formula from A3 into the next ten cells of column A.

4 In cell B2 type **1.** This is the first bacteria.

5 In cell B3 type **= B2*2**.

6 Paste the formula from B3 into the next ten cells in column B.

9 Paste the graph into Write Away! and write an explanation of the curve.

10 If 10 000 bacteria equal one gram, graph the increasing weight of the bacteria in column B using a formula in column C.

Lesson Link | Maths

Square numbers

1 Complete a spreadsheet like this to show the square of each number.

2 In cell B2 type =A2*A2.

3 Paste the formula from B2 into the next nine cells of column B.

4 Predict what shape a line graph of this information will look like.

5 Highlight column A and B.

6 Click  and to see a scatter graph.

Change column A to big numbers – you might be surprised with the graph you get.

Lesson Link | Geography

Population growth

▶ In 1900 the population of a village in Devon was 100 people.

▶ Every 10 years the population was counted. On average, 15 people were born and 8 people died.

Use a spreadsheet to work out how long it would take for the original population to double.

Off Screen

A wise man once said he would have as a reward from the king one penny on the first square of a chessboard, two pennies on the second square and four pennies on the third. He asked the king to continue doubling the pennies on each of the 64 squares. Was the wise man's advice expensive or cheap?

Graphing area

NumberBox 2

Spreadsheets can be used to calculate areas enclosed by fixed perimeters

Check that decimals are shown. Before entering data click **Format** and then click **Type** and then check the decimal box. You may decide not to show decimals in the mousetrap problem.

Skills To Learn | Using shapes to frame text

Fixed perimeter

❯ A farmer has 100 metres of fence.

❯ She wants to enclose the biggest possible area with her fence in a square or rectangular shape.

Use a spreadsheet to help you calculate the most efficient rectangular shape.

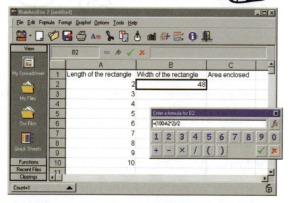

1 In cell B2 type =(100−A2*2)/2.

The formula in B2 doubles the length of the rectangle and takes it away from 100 to see how much fence is left for the width.

It is divided by 2 because 2 widths of fencing are needed.

2 Paste the formula from B2 into the next ten cells of column B.

3 In cell C2 type =A2*B2.

4 Paste the formula from C2 into the next ten cells in column C.

5 Enter different lengths into column A.
- Which is the best rectangle?
- Which is the worst rectangle?

6 Change the length of the fence and see if that has any effect.

Lesson Link — Maths

Area of complex shapes

1 Set up a spreadsheet to calculate the area of shapes which can be split into two or more rectangles.

> Work out the area of each part of my room and write a formula to add them together.

Lesson Link — Technology

Fixed area

> I am starting a mousetrap business.

- Each mousetrap is 12 cm x 10 cm.
- The planks are 100 cm x 20 cm.

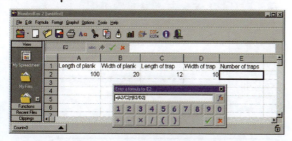

1 In cell E2 type =(A2/C2)*(B2/D2).

> This works out how many mousetraps I can get from each plank.

2 Alter the length and width of each trap to see how many can then be made from each plank.

3 If planks cost £2.75 each, add a column to work out how much each trap will cost.

Off Screen

- Draw some identical circles, all touching but not overlapping.
- How many other circles is each one touching?
- What regular polygon does this remind you of?

- Try tessellating with this regular polygon.
- What natural shapes do these tessellations remind you of?
- Research into the areas enclosed by different polygons.

Scaling and ratios

NumberBox 2

Spreadsheets can be used to scale up amounts and calculate ratios

Check that decimals are shown. Before entering data click **Format** and then click **Type** and then check the decimal box.

Skills To Learn | Adapting recipes

Cake recipe

Paste formulae into rows 3 and 4 to calculate how much of each ingredient you will need for the different numbers of people.

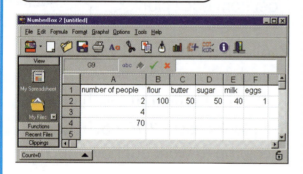

Rate for the job

▸ Three children work together washing cars.

▸ They charge £2.20 for each car.

▸ They divide the money in a ratio according to how old each is.

- Jim 8 years
- Ellie 10 years
- Fran 12 years

That means there will be a total of 30 shares to be divided in the ratio between the children.

Example

1 In cell D2 type **=(B2*C2)*8/30**.

(B2*C2) is the total amount earned by all the children.

8/30 is the fraction of the total earned by Jim.

Complete the chart.

1 Using the ages of Ellie and Fran, work out how much they will earn.

Lesson Link | Maths

Petrol consumption

▶ This is how far these cars go on one litre of petrol:

- MX5 goes 7 miles
- Jaguar XJS goes 3 miles
- Ferrari goes 2 miles
- Yaris goes 9 miles

1 Add formulae to this spreadsheet to work out the distance each can travel on a tankful of petrol and how much it will cost.

2 Change the cost per litre in column B to see what effect it has.

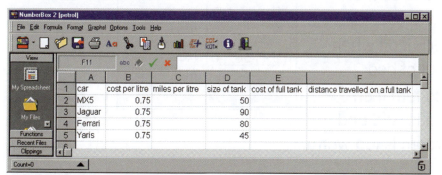

	A	B	C	D	E	F
1	car	cost per litre	miles per litre	size of tank	cost of full tank	distance travelled on a full tank
2	MX5	0.75		50		
3	Jaguar	0.75		90		
4	Ferrari	0.75		80		
5	Yaris	0.75		45		

Lesson Link | Technology

Slippers

▶ To make a single slipper in technology each group was given:

- A4 card
- one sheet of fabric 25 cm square
- 10 cm of fur for decoration
- 20 ml of glue

1 Design a spreadsheet to calculate how much of each resource the teacher would need to provide for different numbers of groups.

2 Put a column in the spreadsheet to show what each group would need to make two slippers.

Off Screen

▶ Open a tube of Smarties and check the ratio of the different colours.

▶ Is this ratio constant in other tubes?

Control

Computers can monitor physical factors

The first activity on cross-curricular links is a revision of an activity in book 5.

| **Skills To Learn** | Using a computer to control devices |

Central heating

▌ We use two ways to control central heating. We use:

- a timer to switch it off when we are in or out of bed
- a thermostat to turn it on when the room is cold and off when the room is too warm.

What controls?

▌ Complete this table.

Device	Which factors in the environment turn it on and off?
street lights	
automatic doors in shops	
smoke alarms	
fire sprinklers	
the motor in a fridge	
movement sensitive security lights	
automatic garage doors	

Lesson Link | Technology

Buzzer

❱ Use the control software.

❱ Build a simple sequence to make a buzzer sound.

```
BUILD buzz
REPEAT
SWITCH ON 1
WAIT 10
SWITCH OFF 1
AGAIN
END
```

to computer

Control

input   output

> To make this run, simply type **DO buzz**.

Lesson Link | Technology

Control the buzzer with an input.

❱ The control box has two rows of inputs.

❱ Plug a wire into each socket of one of the pairs.

❱ If you touch them together the computer thinks the input is on.

❱ This sequence sounds the buzzer only if the two input wires are touching.

```
BUILD switch
REPEAT 100
IF INPUT 1 ON THEN
REPEAT
SWITCH ON 1
WAIT 10
SWITCH OFF 1
AGAIN
END
```

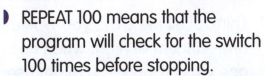

❱ REPEAT 100 means that the program will check for the switch 100 times before stopping.

Off Screen

❱ Some people say that in the future we will have homes which are even more automatic than they are now.

> Design a home with as many automatic features as possible.

Alarms

 PawPrints

A sensor can cause a switch to turn on or off

If control equipment is not available, use the switches to turn on lights and buzzers.

Skills To Learn | Use a variety of sensors to control switches

Either switch

You have been employed to protect some valuable Krypton crystals.

If any one of the sensors was turned on then the alarm would sound.

1 Think of all the ways you would protect them at night when no-one was around. You might use:
- body heat sensors
- vibration sensors
- sensors to detect if the windows were opened
- sensors to detect if a door opens
- a switch to detect if someone was treading near the crystals.

2 Use PawPrints to map the room where they are kept.

3 Show the positions of doors and windows.

4 Draw your detectors on the map.

5 Write a small text box next to each sensor describing how it would work.

Lesson Link Technology

Make two switches to protect the Krypton crytstals.

Switch 1: Use a reed switch.

▶ This type of switch comes on if a magnet is near it.

▶ Connect the wires attached to the reed switch to input 1 sockets.

Switch 2: Use a tilt switch.

▶ In this type of switch, a foil-covered ball rolls down a tube to connect the two wires.

▶ Connect the wires attached to the tilt switch to input 2 sockets.

▶ Plug a buzzer into output 1 and a lamp into output 2.

```
BUILD alarm
REPEAT 100
IF INPUT 1 ON OR IF INPUT 2 ON
THEN
REPEAT
SWITCH ON 1
SWITCH ON 2
WAIT 10
SWITCH OFF 1
SWITCH OFF 2
AGAIN
END
```

This program will sound the alarm if either switch is turned on.

Refine the sequence.

▶ Change the procedure so that the alarm will sound and flash only when both inputs are on.

▶ Change the sequence so that the tilt switch makes the light flash and the reed switch makes the buzzer sound.

▶ This will tell security where to look.

Off Screen English

Write about a raid on the Krypton storage firm

▶ from the point of view of security and the ways they tried to protect the valuable rocks.

▶ from the point of view of the raiders who were trying to steal them. What did they do to try to get round all the detectors and sensors?

Light sensors

Control

Use an if command to turn on a switch

Pupil's will need to understand that a switch will only turn on when a condition such as light level or temperature has been met. They could list ways in which these devices are used to control traffic systems.

Skills To Learn | Use a variety of sensors to control devices

Inputs

As well as simple switches the control box will use light, sound and heat sensors.

Note when the light came on and went off. This is the light level at which the light sensor flips between off and on.

1 Plug the light sensor into a pair of inputs.

2 Type this sequence.

    BUILD test

    REPEAT 100

    IF INPUT 1 ON THEN

    REPEAT

    SWITCH ON 1

    AGAIN

    END

3 Type 'Run test'.

4 Do the same for the other sensors.

5 Explain where these sensors are used in everyday life.

light sensor

light

Lesson Link | Technology

A cool breeze

1 Set up a heat sensor. Plug it into the input 1 sockets.

2 Build a procedure so that a cooling fan is turned on when the temperature is high.

3 Use a table lamp or a beaker of warm water to heat up the detector.

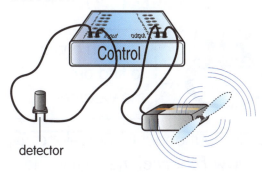

detector

You will need to experiment to get the right level – some sensors will go up in numbers, others will turn on and off.

4 Type in this sequence:

BUILD breeze
REPEAT 100
IF TEMPERATURE > 30 THEN
SWITCH ON 1
IF TEMPERATURE < 30 THEN
SWITCH OFF 1
AGAIN
END

Lesson Link | Technology

Turn that light on.

1 Set up a light detector. Plug it into the input 1 sockets.

2 Build a procedure so that a bulb is turned on when it gets dark.

3 Use a bright torch to help provide bright light.

4 Add another detector which works when a pressure pad is trodden on.

Off Screen

A perfect greenhouse

❭ Use your knowledge of the conditions that plants like to design a system to create the perfect greenhouse. You will need to think about:
  • light
  • heat
  • water
  • ventilation

What is the internet?

Information can be gained from internet sites

A range of short articles from books, CD-ROMs and the internet should be examined and their main points summarised, before working with the internet directly. Pupils should be encouraged to read CD-ROMs or the internet article before copying and printing the relevant selected parts.

Skills To Learn | To log on to an internet site

- The internet is an international network of computers, which are permanently linked by high-speed telephone lines. You link to the internet by hooking your home or school computer to one of these linked computers.

- Your computer is linked to the internet by a company which is an Internet Service Provider (ISP).

- The World Wide Web (WWW) is a store of information on web pages which are available through the internet. Pages on the web are linked by hyperlinks which are text or pictures forming links between pages on the web. Links will often be coloured and will change colour once used.

- Each site on the WWW has an address called an URL (Uniform Resource Locator). The URL for the Natural History Museum in London is www.nhm.ac.uk

Let's get started!

1 Click on the ISP logo on your computer to log on to the web.

Click on a web link to find out about the weather.

2 Find out about FC Barcelona. Type www.fcbarcelona.com in the URL address box and tap ⏎Enter.

3 Find out about Formula One, by searching on a search engine:

- www.google.co.uk
- www.altavista.co.uk

Lesson Link | Geography

Find a map.

1 Go to www.multimap.com

2 Enter the postcode of your school or home.

3 Decide which scale of map you would need to:

- send directions to a friend who lives 200 miles away.

- use when going for a cycle to an attraction two miles away.

- plan a route to take Granny for a walk next time she visits.

4 Import a page of multimap showing roads. Write next to it the directions from a motorway junction to a particular location.

Lesson Link | History

Stonehenge visit

1 Go to the English Heritage website. www.english-heritage.org.uk

2 Click **Places to Visit & Events** .

3 Search for information about Stonehenge.

4 Write notes to remind you of:

- costs
- the hours they are open
- how to get there
- the history of Stonehenge.

5 Look through the rest of the English Heritage site to plan more visits to tourist attractions close to where you live.

Off Screen

Use a photocopied page from a book about the internet which tells you how to search for what you want. Use different colours to underline useful information, e.g. use green to underline good sites to visit.

Using a favourites list

To access an internet site using a favourites list

It is a great help if you prepare this list of favourites (Bookmarks in Netscape), before the start of the lesson.

Skills To Learn | Picking sites for study

▶ When you have visited an interesting site you might want to store the address so you can visit it easily next time. Netscape Navigator uses Bookmarks and Microsoft Explorer uses Favourites.

Add a website to your favourites.

1 Go to the BBC website, www.bbc.co.uk.

2 Click [Favorites].

3 Click [Add...].

4 Click [OK].

Internet Explorer already has folders set up for you to organise your favourites.

Open a website from your favourites.

1 Click [Favorites].

2 Select the website you want to look at.

This is a list of favourites. Choose one of these and explore the site.

▶ If these sites are not actually on your computer just type the address (URL) in the address box.

- www.exploratorium.edu
- www.bbc.co.uk
- www.homeworkhigh.co.uk
- www.ubl.com
- www.manutd.co.uk

This is just one football club site. Use search engines to go to the site of your favourite team.

Lesson Link Science

Here is a list of science favourites. Print any page you want to read again.

▸ www.fourmilab.ch.earthview/vplanet.html
This views the Earth showing its present position along with the sun's light and shadow.

▸ www.NASA.gov
The biggest source of information on things about space.

▸ http://volcano.und.nodak.edu

▸ www.bbc.co.uk/revisewise/science

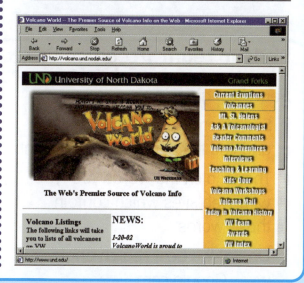

Lesson Link English

Here is a list of favourite authors' sites. Bookmark them so they are easy to find next time.

▸ www.judyblume.com/main-menu
Find out about Judy Blume.

▸ www.cslewis.drzeus.net
Visit the Into the Wardrobe site.

▸ www.roalddahlfans.com/
Read about Roald Dahl.

▸ www.kidsread.com/harrypotter/jkrowling
Read about J.K.Rowling.

Off Screen

▸ Use post-it notes to mark the places in an encyclopaedia where you found interesting information.

These are especially useful if you write on the note what it is marking.

Use a search engine

Use a search engine to find information

Children could try using identical searches with different search engines and compare the results. Alta-Vista and Yahoo are good ones to try.

Skills To Learn | Learn to use a search engine

Search engines

▶ Search engines explore the web and find the information you want.

▶ They match the words you type with web sites which contain those words.

▶ One of the best search engines is www.Google.com

City search

1 Open Google.

2 Type the name of one big city in the search box.

3 Click [Google Search].

4 Count the number of hits.

5 Make a list of the cities you search for and the number of hits you get.

6 Do cities in any part of the world get more hits than others?

7 Why do you think that New York gets more hits than Calcutta even though the Indian city is much bigger?

Village or town search

1 Type in the name of a small town or village you know.

2 Have a competition to try to find a village or town with fewer than three hits!

Lesson Link | History

History searches

1 Open Google.

2 Type in the name of the period you are studying in history.

3 Click [Google Search].

4 Skim the list of entries.

5 Which ones look most interesting?

6 Click [Favorites] and click [Add...] to bookmark the sites which look worth visiting again.

Lesson Link | Music

Music searches

1 Open Google.

2 Type in the name of a musical instrument you like listening to.

3 Which sites look most interesting?

Make a music favourites folder.

1 Find a music page you like.

2 Click [Favorites] and click [Add...].

3 Click [Create in >>].

4 Click [New Folder...].

5 Give your folder a name.

6 Click [OK].

Song words

1 Open Google.

2 Type in the name of a pop group you want to find out about.

Off Screen

▶ Look in your local Yellow Pages.

▶ Which category has most entries? (just estimate – do not count!)

Which categories have at least one entry but fewer than five?

Smarter searching

**Use complex searches
to locate information**

Looking at web pages is also
known as 'surfing the web'.
Searches can be time-
consuming, frustrating and
unproductive if they are too
vague. They may also turn up
unexpected sites of interest.

Skills To Learn | Get the information you want from a search

Better searches

1 Open Google.

2 Type Paris in the search box.

3 Click [Google Search].

There are over
15,000,000 hits!

If you only want to find out about
the Eiffel Tower in Paris, you need
to make the search narrower.

4 Type Eiffel Tower Paris in the
search box.

5 Click [Google Search].

This has narrowed
the search down
to 115,000 hits.

Plus and minus

❭ There are a number of ways to
help refine your searches.

- + signs tell the search engine
to finds web sites which contain
that word.

- - signs tell the search engine to
ignore any web pages which
contain that word.

❭ If you wanted to find out about
places to visit in Paris but did not
want information on the Eiffel
Tower, you need to type:
+Paris +Tours -Eiffel

Plan your own.

Plan your own searches to find:

- information about towers in
England which are not on castles

- a map of the Paris Metro.

Lesson Link | Maths

Fun sites

There are many fun sites on the web for maths games and puzzles.

1 Open Google.
2 Type maths+puzzles+games +children in the search box.
3 Click [Google Search].

I found sites like this.

▶ www.kidspsych.org/pyramid.html
▶ www.coolmath4kids.com/ numbermonster
▶ www.cadburylearningzone.co.uk/ maths/

Lesson Link | English

Witch search

▶ The three witches in Shakespeare's play 'Macbeth' have a famous speech about cauldrons and toads.

▶ Here are some words you might use to find it. Choose three of them and search.
  • Shakespeare, witches, toads, bubble, cauldron, Macbeth, play, three.

Poetry search

1 There is a famous poem by Kipling called 'If'. Can you find it?
2 Edward Lear wrote nonsense poems. Use his name and any of the following words to find some.
  • limerick, pussycat, Pobble, Jumblies, nonsense.
3 Type in the name of your favourite poet. What can you find out about them?

Off Screen

▶ In an anthology of poems search the index for your favourite poem using the title or first line.

▶ Search for poems by your favourite poet. You will find these listed in the index too.

Download from the web

Save pictures and text and import to a document for a presentation Sources should be acknowledged

There are many useful sources of text, data and graphics available for free on the internet. Sometimes whole programs or upgrades are available for free and these are called 'freeware'.

Skills To Learn Copy and paste pictures and text from sites

Copy and paste a picture.

1 Go to a site which has some good pictures.

2 When you see a picture you like, click on it.

3 Click Edit and Copy .

4 Open your word processor.

5 Paste it onto a page.

Save a picture.

1 When you see a picture you want to save on your hard disk, click it with your right mouse button.

2 Click Save Picture As... .

3 Give your file a name and choose where you want to save it.

4 Click Save .

Open Link
Open Link in New Window
Save Target As...
Print Target

Show Picture
Save Picture As...
Set as Wallpaper
Set as Desktop Item...

Cut
Copy
Copy Shortcut
Paste

Add to Favorites...

Properties

Go to a picture store.

1 Open Google and click Images .

2 Type in the pictures you want.

3 Click Google Search .

4 Look through the images on show.

5 Click the one you want.

6 Click Edit and Select All .

7 Click Edit and Copy .

8 Paste the image into your own work and save it.

> Most pictures on the web can be used on your own computer but always write where they came from.

Save words.

1 Select the text you want to save.

2 Click Edit and Copy .

3 Open a word document and paste the words you have copied.

4 Save the new word processor file.

Lesson Link PE

1 Search for a site which will tell you about a game you like playing or watching.

2 Copy some of the words and pictures to help you design your own guide to that game.

3 Remember to credit the sites you used.

4 Find out the differences between the rules for netball and matball.

Type **matball rules** into the Google search window.

Lesson Link RE

1 Use a search engine to find out about creation stories from different cultures.

Type **Creation+Myth** in the search box.

2 Copy the pictures and text you need to make a booklet about creation stories from different cultures.

3 One good site is www.mythinglinks. org/ct~creation.html

Type **Creation+Bible +Adam+Eve** to find out about the creation story in the Bible.

Off Screen

▶ Find books or magazine articles about fun things to make and do.

▶ Photocopy the pages you want.

▶ Make them into a collection of ideas to do on a rainy day.

▶ Add your own ideas.

Glossary

bookmark	Also called favourites, short cut to a site you use often.
column guide	Lines showing the edge of columns.
complex search	Looking for information in a database using more than one question at a time.
control box	A device which turns switches on and off, using the computer.
control software	A program which uses data (inputs) such as temperature or light sensors, and switches (outputs), to control systems such as lights or alarms.
data	Information.
datalogging	Recording information onto the computer using sensors.
device	A machine which does a job.
favourites	Also called bookmark, a short cut to a site you use often.
footer	A section at the foot of a page which will show the same information on every page of a document, e.g. the page number or name of the author.
format	The appearance of text or a page layout.
formula	A calculation
header	A section at the top of a page which will show the same information on every page of a document, e.g. the title/chapter heading.
input	Information received by a computer.
internet	A worldwide computer network made up of smaller networks.
ISP	Internet Service Provider
link	A connection between pages, which will take you from one page to the next when it is clicked on with a mouse.

multimedia	Using computers to combine text, graphics, sound and video images.
OR search	Looking for information in a database using the word OR between questions.
orientation	The way a page is seen. Horizontal layout is landscape. Vertical layout is portrait.
output	Information sent by a computer to control a device.
right click	To click the right mouse button. This usually puts a menu on screen.
search engine	A program which can be used to find pages on the web.
sensor	A device which monitors changes such as temperature, light, or sound.
simulation	A program designed to simulate something in the real world, which would be hard to replicate in reality, e.g. a Roman city or life on a new planet.
slideshow	A file of linked pages containing text/data/graphics combined to create a presentation.
spreadsheet	Rows and columns of data stored in cells.
web site	A set of pages on the internet belonging to one person or organisation.
WWW	The World Wide Web is a store of information pages which are linked electronically and can be accessed using a computer.
URL	A Uniform Resource Locator is the address of a web site. They always start with www.